GAME OF BONES

GAME OF BONES

Bone Broth Cookbook of The Seven Kingdoms

Healing Broths & Hearty Feasts to Die For

Harper McKinney

Copyright © 2017

Harper McKinney

All rights reserved. No part of this publication may be reproduced, distributed, or transmitted in any form or by any means, including photocopying, recording, or other electronic or mechanical methods, without the prior written permission of the publisher, except in the case of brief quotations embodied in critical reviews and certain other non-commercial uses permitted by copyright law.

Disclaimer: This book is in no way affiliated with the official Game of Thrones series, HBO or the A Game of Thrones series of novels by George R.R. Martin. This book contains genuine bone broth recipes written with parodied character and plot references. The author cannot accept responsibility for the reproduction or results of these recipes in your kitchen. Always consult a professional before undertaking a new diet and take due care to educate yourself on this form of cooking.

BEFORE YOU BEGIN

Bonus: Free Cookbooks!

If you are a huge cookbook addict then I'd love to help satiate your appetite for new recipes! As a small token of thanks for picking up this book I'd like to offer you the chance to pick up more just like it for free by joining my cookbook addicts club!

You can find out more at the back of this book. Can't wait that long?

Visit http://geni.us/cookbookaddicts to join the club now!

TABLE OF CONTENTS

BEFORE YOU BEGIN v
    Bonus: Free Cookbooks! v
Introduction 1
I. The Power Within 5
II. Essential Broths & Stocks 7
    Khal's Stock 8
    Joff's Beef Broth 10
    Blackwater Broth 12
    Poultry in Motion 14
    Brienne's Helping Hand 16
    Cat's Pork Broth 17
    Braavosi Chicken Broth 18
    Oberyn's Duck Delight 20
    Yara's Fish Bone Broth 22
    Hodor's Rabbit Remedy 24
III. Sipping Beverages 27
    Siblings' Smoothie 28
    Ygritte's Chicken Brew 29
    Restorative Ginger Chicken 30
    Gregor's Fury 31
    Cersei's Fish Elixir 32

IV. Of Beast and Bird 35

Lannister Hot Pot 36

Rejuvenating Red Meat 38

Humble Pie 40

Three-Eyed Stir-Fry 42

Pious Pork Chops 44

Bear's Beef Stew 46

Ramsay's Beef Chili 48

Homecoming Chicken Pie 50

Friendzone Casserole 52

Benjen's Chicken & Bacon Breakfast 54

Valhar Meatballis 55

Petyr's Chicken Patties 56

V. From Land And Sea 59

Iron Islands Halibut 60

Dragons' Tilapia Treat 62

Selyse's Spicy Lemon Haddock 64

Bone-Setting Soup 66

Olenna's Veg Risotto 68

Sam's Sweet Potato 69

Bronn's Baked Fennel 70

Unburnt Kale 72

VI. Sweet Things 75

Tywin's Muffins 76

Dany's Blueberry Sweet Bread 77

Tyrion's Trusty Truffles 78

Resurrection Pound Cake 79

Waffles for Serious People 80

Bone Broth Mistakes 83

Measurement Conversions 87

Liquids, Herbs & Spices 88

Common Non-Liquids by Weight 89

Weight Conversions 90

Get Your BONUS 92

Free Cookbooks 92

Like This Book? 93

About The Author 95

INTRODUCTION

The Seven Kingdoms were not built on a diet of kale and coconut milk. The Mountain didn't make his name by nibbling on nuts and seeds. The Iron Throne will NEVER be taken by a VEGAN!

The men and women of Westeros and Essos were made tough from the moment they were plucked from the teat. These people wasted none of the animals they hunted and cooked, right down to their very bones.

It was this secret that allowed them to forge warriors as formidable as Khal Drogo, Gregor Clegane, Ygritte of the Free Folk and the hero that is Jon Snow. These powerhouses were raised on a diet rich in the proteins and minerals found deep within the bones of the animals they roamed the lands with.

This cookbook contains essential broths and stocks that you can enjoy right away or use for cooking later on. There's also plenty of sipping beverages for those who are constantly on the go, marching their armies through enemy territory of doing the school run.

And then, of course, there's the feasts; a collection of hearty main meal recipes to die for, each of which goes perfectly with your new bone broth stocks.

All of this is topped off by a collection of sweet things; delicious desserts with a bone broth twist. Altogether there are offerings of beast, bird, fish, vegetables and treats enough to fill even the greatest feasting halls of the Seven Kingdoms.

Why no pretty pictures? Because proper people are more concerned with how their food tastes and performs than how it looks.

Do you think the men of the Night's Watch or the women from the land beyond The Wall wasted time preening and primping so they could share their creations with other tribes? Of course not!

By the time you have finished with your hashtags and filters the dish will have gone cold or been stolen by intrepid raiders. So you are encouraged to cook with heart and enjoy your broths and feasts just as Sandor Clegane enjoys a good chicken!

If you too want to become a formidable fighter, tame dragons, stake a claim for the Iron Throne, or simply stave off the common cold, then read on. The recipes and remedies packed into this magical cookbook will create a stronger, better you. It is known.

"THERE IS A CHEF IN EVERY MAN, AND IT STIRS WHEN YOU PUT A SPATULA IN HIS HAND."

I. THE POWER WITHIN

The first men made use of every part of the beasts they hunted and slew. Bones, marrow, feet, tendons, muscles, ligaments and all. The Maesters knew the powers within each and every one of these precious components and allowed nothing to go to waste.

Calcium, collagen, glutamine, magnesium, phosphorous, silicone, glycine. The list goes on, and benefits range from improving joint health and reducing inflammation, to boosting the immune system, healing leaky gut syndrome and overcoming food intolerances and allergies.

The would-be Queens among you will also be glad to know that this ancient practice can even reduce cellulite and boost your skin health. It's easy to see, then, why this magical culinary technique has been passed down through the oral histories from the First Men, to the Andals and beyond.

Some vendors have tried to take advantage of this by manufacturing synthetic stocks and broths, but these are a pale and ineffective imitation. If you want to grow healthy, strong and vibrant then you need the real thing.

If you are too posh to hunt your own animals, make sure you purchase only grass-fed organic beasts and not those packed with chemicals, otherwise your joy will turn to ashes in your mouth.

You now hold an ancient secret in your hands, and possess the power to fulfill your destiny. To ensure you stay safe and maximize your results, it is recommended to check out the 5 common bone broth mistakes towards the back of the book before you proceed. After all, with great power comes great responsibility.

II. ESSENTIAL BROTHS & STOCKS

It all begins with these simple, ancient remedies, ready to be taken as they are or stored and used as stocks for feasts later on.

KHAL'S STOCK

The first thing Daenerys Targaryen discovered when she married the mighty Khal was that apart from the occasional horse heart, he really liked to start each morning with a cup of bone broth.

So, she learned the following recipe from the old Dothraki women to get into his good graces. She also learned a little something in the bedroom, but this isn't that kind of book.

Serves: 16 | Prep Time: 10 mins | Cooking Time: 8 hours

Ingredients

- 4 chicken feet
- 2.5-3 pounds animal bones left over from a feast
- 2-3 tablespoons apple cider vinegar
- 3 carrots
- 1 zucchini
- 2 onions
- Large bunch of parsley leaves
- 2 teaspoons dried thyme
- 1 tablespoon salt

Directions

1. With the help of the Khalasar wives, she placed all the bones in a large pot. You may enlist the help of your family or friends.

2. Cover the bones with water, filling the pot, and add the vinegar to draw out the magic inside. Leave to sit for about half an hour.

3. Take an arakh (Dothraki sword) and chop the vegetables. Put them into the pot.

4. After that, place the pot over a vigorous fire or, if you're high born, an electric cooker, and wait until it begins to bubble.

5. Let the fire burn low and allow the broth to cook for about 8 hours.

6. Carefully remove all the foam that forms periodically using a large spoon.

7. In the last half an hour, add the chopped parsley to taste.

8. Strain the broth and pour into sealable jars.

You can fill a drinking horn with this nectar and enjoy the benefits right away, or keep it in the fridge for up to 5 days. The other option is to freeze it for later use, or use it as a stock.

So, now you know how to make a broth fit for a King and Queen. What's that Jorah? Oh right, of course, sorry, Khal and Khaleesi. Sheesh.

JOFF'S BEEF BROTH

Even Cersei understood that her first son was a misogynistic sadist who loved nothing more than hurting people. Hoping she could help him become a better ruler, she started feeding him bone broth every day.

She learned the recipe from an old witch who swore by it. So, if you want to draw out the good in a person, prepare this recipe and serve them with a cup each day.

Serves: 14-16 | Prep Time: 10 mins | Cooking Time: 48 hours

Ingredients

- 3.5-4 pounds of beef bones (which also contain marrow)
- 2 celery stalks
- 2 medium celeriac
- 2 carrots
- 2 parsley roots
- 3 yellow onion
- ¼ cup apple cider vinegar (from Maester Qyburn's potions)
- 1 bay leaf
- 1 teaspoon black peppercorns
- 2 bell peppers
- 1 teaspoon dried thyme
- 1 teaspoon dried oregano
- Small bunch of fresh parsley

Directions

1. Roughly chop all the veggies, or ask someone else to do it if such menial tasks are beneath you.

2. Supposing your kitchen is fancy enough to have a crockpot, place all the ingredients inside.

3. Fill the pot with water and bring it to the boil over a strong fire.

4. Let the fire weaken, and let the stock cook for a day or two.

5. Skim the fat and foam from time to time.

6. When two moons have passed, take out the veg and strain the broth through a fine sieve.

7. Allow the liquid to come to room temperature before you serve it.

Give the broth to those in need of a pick-me-up. You may keep it for seven days in the fridge or about 3 months in the freezer.

However, you should know that it had no effect on Joffrey, as his drinking cup was mistakenly switched on his wedding day.

BLACKWATER BROTH

Everybody knows wine was Tyrion's first love, but bone broth came a close second. Hold up, no, women were probably second. So wine, women, bone broth. Or possibly wine, women, patricide, bone broth. Let's go with that.

In any case, whenever he wanted to keep his mind clear, like for the Battle of the Blackwater, he switched the ruby liquid with a secret potion his nanny used to feed him when he was a child.

Serves: 8 | Prep Time: 10 mins | Cooking Time: 9 ½ - 24 hours

Ingredients

- 4 pounds of short ribs, oxtail, and knuckled bones, combined (Tyrion had Bronn chop them into halves with a cleaver)
- 2 leeks
- 1 celeriac
- 1 head cabbage
- 2 onions
- 4 celery stalks
- 4-5 carrots
- 1 bay leaf
- 2 teaspoons peppercorns
- 1 tablespoon apple cider vinegar
- 7-8 garlic cloves

Directions

1. If you're royalty, you've probably got an oven, so turn it on and set to 450°F.

2. Use a hand size blade to cut all the vegetables, and place them near the bones on a large baking tray.

3. Take the tray to the oven and bake for about half an hour, stirring after the first 10 minutes.

4. Transfer the contents of the dish to a large stockpot and cover with about 12 cups of water, or more if needed. Tyrion was always tempted to add a cup of red wine too, but do try to resist, at least until serving time.

5. Add the remaining ingredients.

6. Place the pot over an intense flame until it begins to boil.

7. Set the fire on low and cook for up to a full day, but for at least 9 hours, removing the foam once in a while.

8. Remove the veg and strain the broth using a colander.

9. Let cool before drinking.

You may keep the remaining broth in the fridge for about 5 days or freeze it for use within 6 months.

You will most certainly feel sharper and smarter after drinking this beverage. Unfortunately it does nothing for your British accent, though.

POULTRY IN MOTION

People in the North had to eat hearty to stave off the long winter plagues. All the bones left from their meals were used to prepare an ancient beverage that coursed through their veins like liquid courage. No wonder Robb Stark was on such a hot streak.

All the women gathered to prepare this mighty bone broth for the fearless Stark bannermen after their victory over the Lannister army. Do the same, and you too could become a heroic monarch venerated by the bards. Or perhaps just a mildly appreciated parent.

Serves: 14-16 | Prep Time: 10 mins | Cooking Time: 48 hours

Ingredients

- 4-5 pounds poultry wings (or necks and feet)
- 2 yellow onions
- 2 carrots
- 2 zucchinis
- 1 celeriac
- 1 green bell pepper
- 2 parsnips
- 6 garlic cloves
- 4 tablespoons apple cider vinegar
- Small bunch of fresh parsley
- 1 teaspoon black peppercorns
- 2 teaspoons sea salt (from Theon's reserves)
- 2 sprigs fresh thyme
- 2 sprigs fresh rosemary

Directions

1. Hack the vegetables into large pieces with a sharp blade.

2. Place all the ingredients in the biggest pot you have.

3. Pour water over the meat and veggies, and watch until the broth begins to boil over an intense flame.

4. Reduce the fire, and leave the broth to cook for about two days.

5. Meanwhile, you may continue planning military strategies; just remember to take away the impurities that gather at the surface from time to time.

6. When the stock has chilled, strain it and serve your army.

If there is some broth left, keep it in the fridge for a week or freeze it for use within 3 months.

Robb Stark enjoyed this beverage greatly. It put curls in his hair, a spring in his step and a dagger in his belly. Oh no, wait, that was Roose Bolton. Damn it Roose.

BRIENNE'S HELPING HAND

Jaime Lannister was devastated when he lost his hand: not only would he never again fight like a true warrior, but he couldn't even chop his vegetables! Lady Brienne, who was not-so-secretly in love with him, took pity on the man and taught him this simple recipe, no chopping required.

Serves: 8 | Prep Time: 5 mins | Cooking Time: 24 hours

Ingredients

- 2-3 pounds animal bones (beef or chicken)
- 1 teaspoon salt
- 1 tablespoon black peppercorns
- 2 tablespoons apple cider vinegar

Directions

1. Place all the ingredients into a slow cooker or stockpot.
2. Fill the pot with water.
3. Light the fire and watch until the water begins to bubble.
4. Set the fire on low and simmer the broth for about one day. Put on some seductive music and polish your best armor.
5. After it has cooled down, discard all the bones and any other remaining solids.
6. Serve a cup per day to heal your body.

Use the leftover broth within a week if refrigerated, or place in the freezer to add to other lovely recipes later.

They say the best way to a man's heart is through his stomach, so we may yet see a love story unfold before the game is up!

CAT'S PORK BROTH

Don't worry, it's not made *of* cat; it's made *by* Cat! Catelyn Stark was a fiercely devoted mother to her children, and she loved them tremendously. She knew that Northern kids needed proper nutrition, and did her best to provide them with the best foods she could, even though 'attachment parenting' was not so fashionable back then.

One of her finest recipes, inherited from her great-grandmother, was a delicious pork bone broth. She even cooked it the day King Robert and the Lannisters came to Winterfell. Rumor has it Bran stole Jaime's serving, and the rest is history.

Serves: 8-12 | Prep Time: 5 mins | Cooking Time: 4 hours

Ingredients

- 2 pounds pork leg bones
- 1 piece fresh ginger root (about 2 inches)
- 2-3 tablespoons medium-dry sherry
- 2 lemongrass stalks

Directions

1. Ask the local butcher to chop the bones into 3-4 pieces.
2. Place the bones into a large pot and add the other ingredients.
3. Cover with water until the pot is almost full.
4. Light a fire beneath it and wait until the water reaches boiling point.
5. Set the flame on low and simmer for about 4 hours, skimming the foam from time to time.
6. If you check the pot and see that there is not enough water, heat some more and pour over the bones.
7. Strain the broth using a fine colander.

If you don't happen to be hosting royalty and have some broth left over, keep it in the fridge for 10-14 days or in the freezer for 2 months.

Just be sure to make enough to go around, and place your guests on the ground floor, just in case.

BRAAVOSI CHICKEN BROTH

Arya Stark has been through some stuff, man. Just after killing Ser Meryn Trant, when she thought that everything might finally be taking a turn for the better, she was stricken with blindness.

Some may consider this a punishment for overruling the will of the Many-Faced God, but Arya considered it a challenge, and started to seek out other sensations.

She stumbled upon (get it?) a recipe for a secret potion that can make people see things the way they never did before. If you need clarity in your life, follow this recipe.

Serves: 4 | Prep Time: 5 mins | Cooking Time: 12 hours

Ingredients

- 1 pound chicken wings or feet
- 4-5 hot chili peppers
- 1 piece of fresh ginger (approximately 2 inches thick)
- 1 teaspoon turmeric powder
- 1 star anise
- 1 lemongrass stalk
- 2-3 green onions
- Juice from 2 lemons
- Few sprigs of fresh mint (from sunny Braavos)

Directions

1. It was quite easy for Arya to prepare this broth, despite being blind. You don't have to do anything complicated, just add all the ingredients to a large pot.

2. Cover everything with water and put the lid on.

3. When the water comes to the boil, reduce the heat and continue cooking for up to half a day.

4. Add some more water from time to time if needed.

5. Occasionally remove any impurities that may reach the surface.

6. Remove any solids, and strain until you get a clear broth.

Keep the stock in the fridge for a few days or in the freezer for later use.

By drinking this broth every day, Arya eventually recovered from her condition, but unfortunately, she was still followed everywhere by the Stark luck.

OBERYN'S DUCK DELIGHT

Knowing the Red Viper's preference for exotic tastes, Ellaria Sand decided to prepare a special broth before her lover's big fight with The Mountain.

She opted for a duck bone broth; flavored with the herbs she found in King's Landing's produce markets. She came back with a basket full of goodies. You can prepare the same broth if you follow this recipe.

Serves: 18-20 | Prep Time: 20 mins | Cooking Time: 6 hours

Ingredients

- 5-6 wild duck carcasses (or 2 domestic ducks if you are not such a good hunter)
- ½ oz. dried mushrooms (wild ones are the best, but not too wild, or you'll end up like Joffrey)
- 2 carrots
- 2 fennel bulbs (only tops)
- 2 celeriac
- 3 celery stalks
- 2 yellow bell peppers
- 2 onions
- 1 zucchini
- 1 handful of fresh parsley
- Few sprigs of rosemary
- Few sage leaves
- Few sprigs of fresh thyme
- Few sprigs of fresh oregano
- 2 bay leaves
- 1 tablespoon peppercorns
- 2-3 scallions
- 1 tablespoon salt
- Olive oil for brushing

Directions

1. Brush all the carcasses with oil.

2. Light the oven and set to 400°F. Place the bones on a baking tray and roast for about 60 minutes. Meanwhile, you may enjoy a cup of fine wine from sunny Dorne.

3. Break the bones into smaller pieces, and place them into the largest stockpot you have.

4. Roughly cut all the veggies, and bring them to the pot together with the herbs and salt.

5. Cover the ingredients with water, and set atop the stove fire.

6. When the water starts to bubble, reduce the heat.

7. Cook the stock for about 4-6 hours and remember to skim the impurities.

8. Remove all the solids with a large spoon and strain the liquid.

9. Let the broth cool down and serve.

You may either keep it in the fridge for 6-7 days or in the freezer for up to 9 months.

This concoction is said to infuse the recipient with unshakeable confidence. Unfortunately for Prince Oberyn, his mistress may have overdone it a little in that department.

YARA'S FISH BONE BROTH

When she staked her claim to the Salt Throne of the Iron Islands, Yara Greyjoy was unable to convince the men of the Kingsmoot. But the Princess had a secret that she hoped would help her win their favor.

The ace up her sleeve was a recipe for fish bone broth she had learned on the seas. It is said that this drink can provide so many vitamins, minerals and good fats that it can add a backbone to any meal. Too bad it couldn't provide one for her brother. Heyo!

Serves: 16 | Prep Time: 15 mins | Cooking Time: 90 mins

Ingredients

- 6-7 pounds of fish carcasses (from the fishermen of the Iron Islands)
- 2 onions
- 2 carrots
- 2 medium celeriacs
- 2 bay leaves
- 2 parsnips
- 1 parsley root
- 1 teaspoon black peppercorn
- Small bunch of parsley leaves
- 2 tablespoons ghee
- 1 teaspoon dried oregano

Directions

1. Chop the vegetables, taking care that Theon is not around when you do the carrot.
2. Place the ghee in a stockpot and heat until it melts.
3. Sauté the veg for 17-18 minutes until they begin to soften.
4. Add the carcasses, and cover with water.
5. When the water begins to slightly bubble, remove the impurities from the surface.
6. Stir in the peppercorns, bay leaves, oregano, and parsley.
7. Continue to cook for about 50-60 minutes.
8. Strain to get rid of all the solids, and let cool.

Keep the broth in the fridge if you plan to use it within a week. If you put it in the freezer, you can use it for about ninety days.

Although Yara didn't prevail at the Kingsmoot, she still came out stronger than her brother. Which is still a pretty serious win, as any sisters out there will know.

HODOR'S RABBIT REMEDY

Hodor was an active child who loved to go hunting. He always came back with a brace of rabbits from the surrounding woods. His mother gave the meat to the castle cook, but kept the bones and carcasses to make a special broth for her son.

All the precious substances from the stock helped the boy grow strong, and made such an impression on the gentle giant that before long all he could say was "bone broth!"

Serves: 4 | Prep Time: 5 mins | Cooking Time: 2 ½ hours

Ingredients

- 1 ½ pound rabbit bones
- ½ cup tomato puree
- 2 carrots
- 1 onion
- 1 parsnip
- 1 small celeriac
- 1 tablespoon black peppercorns
- ¼ cup dry wine
- Small bunch of fresh dill
- 1 teaspoon dried oregano

Directions

1. Chop all the bones into smaller pieces with a cleaver.
2. Chop the veggies.
3. Place the bones into a small cauldron and cover with water, and then place over a cooking fire.
4. When the water begins to bubble, remove all the foam from the surface.
5. Cook for about half an hour, and then add all the vegetables and spices.
6. Let the flame subside and simmer for about 2 ½ hours.
7. Strain the stock and sip away.

Store the rabbit broth in the fridge for no more than one week or freeze it for later when you might need it.

Legend has it that the walkers who entered the cave where Hodor, Bran, Osha and Meera were resting were trying to get hold of the recipe. There was no way in hell that the big man was about to let that happen.

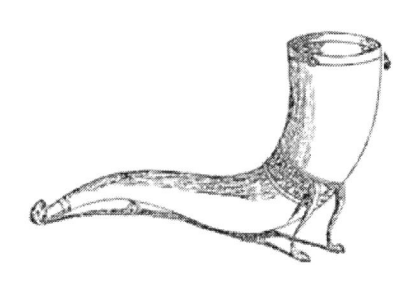

III. SIPPING BEVERAGES

For those days when you need a quick and easy remedy, these delicious drinks will provide the power you need to take on the Seven Kingdoms.

SIBLINGS' SMOOTHIE

When Jon and Sansa were reunited after so long spent apart, the siblings were both so incredibly touched that they could barely contain their tears. However, there was a sense of unease about who was to be the new head of Winterfell.

It was decided that whichever of the two could finish this ancient green smoothie packed with nourishing magic first would effectively rule the land. OK that's not strictly true, but the kids don't need to know that.

Serves: 2 | Prep Time: 5 mins | Cooking Time: 0

Ingredients

- 2 cups beef bone broth
- 2 cups kale leaves
- ½ cup fresh parsley
- 1 lemon

Directions

1. Place the bone broth in a pot and heat through.
2. Transfer to a food processor. Make no mistake; Jon kept a high-speed blender in the kitchen after discovering that Amazon delivered to Winterfell.
3. Squeeze the lemon juice.
4. Add to the blender along with the kale leaves and fresh parsley.
5. Process until smooth.
6. Enjoy while still warm.

Only prepare the amount of sipping beverage that you need. The drink cannot be kept for later since the greens will oxidize and lose all their magical properties.

Turns out this drink didn't solve anything between the brother and sister. I guess we'll have to wait for season seven for that.

YGRITTE'S CHICKEN BREW

Ygritte: "Don't ever betray me."

Jon Snow: "I won't."

Well, this drink might not guarantee you can keep hold of your lover, but it can sure as hell help you get them alone in a cave in the first place.

Nobody knows if the love between Jon Snow and Ygritte would have developed at all if it weren't for a decadent beverage the free woman served Jon on their first night together. You may also prepare this recipe for a special occasion.

Serves: 2 | Prep Time: 5 mins | Cooking Time: None

Ingredients

- 2 cups chicken bone broth
- ½ cup coconut cream
- ½ teaspoon cayenne pepper (to spice up things a little)
- 1 teaspoon grated ginger
- 1 lime

Directions

1. Light a small fire and warm the bone broth.
2. Add to a blender.
3. Squeeze the lime juice and add it to the processor together with the rest of the ingredients.
4. Blend until smooth and extremely tasty.
5. Sip while still warm.

Only prepare the quantity you need for that special occasion. You may also keep it in the fridge for 12-24 hours, but it may change its consistency and taste, just like Jon.

Alas, Snow went back to Castle Black to fulfill his destiny, but he remembered his first taste long after the two parted ways.

RESTORATIVE GINGER CHICKEN

When Khal Drogo was wounded, Daenerys asked Mirri Maz Duur to save him. The slave woman had to find all kinds of ingredients so as to prepare a potion that could bring the mighty Khal back from the brink.

Unfortunately the magic elixir could not prevent Drogo's decline. Of course, the concoction would have nursed a woman back to full health within a matter of minutes, but men always have made a bit more of a fuss.

Serves: 2 | Prep Time: 5 mins | Cooking Time: 0

Ingredients

- 2 cups chicken bone broth
- ½ teaspoon apple cider vinegar
- 1 lemon
- 2 teaspoons grated fresh ginger
- 2 garlic cloves
- ¼ teaspoon cayenne pepper
- 1 tablespoon ghee
- ½ teaspoon ground anise seeds

Directions

1. Set a small fire.
2. Place the bone broth in a small pot and heat through while muttering incantations.
3. Crush the garlic and put it in the pan.
4. Use an old wooden spoon to stir while cackling occasionally.
5. Enjoy the drink as warm as you can.

Keep the remaining beverage in the fridge for one or two days, but make sure to heat it every time you need to drink.

If your cold…sorry…khal flu…fails to vanish immediately after drinking, it might be considered a little excessive to burn whoever made it on a pyre. Give it a few days, at least.

GREGOR'S FURY

As Sandor "The Hound" Clegane found out to his cost, you only steal food from your brother once. Gregor "The Mountain" Clegane does not mess about when it comes to mealtime, and went so far as to acquaint his brother's face with the fire after discovering his sibling had finished off his favorite beverage while he was out killing.

Thankfully the ingredients in this drink helped The Hound maintain a sharp mind and strong joints due to the healthy fats and plenitude of minerals, so although his aspirations of being Westeros' next top model were dealt a blow, he still had a strong career in the King's guard ahead of him.

Serves: 2 | Prep Time: 5 mins | Cooking Time: 0

Ingredients

- 2 cups bone broth (choose from something you made before)
- ½ cup plain yogurt
- 2 tablespoons ghee
- ½ teaspoon freshly ground pepper
- 1 teaspoon kelp powder
- Salt to taste

Directions

1. Light up a fire.
2. Warm the bone broth a little bit and add the ghee. Stir until it melts.
3. Add the other ingredients and stir vigorously.
4. Serve it warm.

You should make sure you drink everything right away, because this drink can't be kept in the fridge with untrustworthy siblings around. Just prepare what you need and do another batch the next day.

Oh and please, remember, this one is not for dogs.

CERSEI'S FISH ELIXIR

Ever since she was a little girl, Cersei has understood the power of beauty. As she grew older, she discovered it was waning slightly and this disturbing revelation sent her into action.

She demanded the bumbling Maester get to work on an elixir of beauty and youth immediately. Such was the power of this secret potion, the Maester firmly insisted that Cersei keep it within the family. Advice she may have taken a little too far.

Serves: 2 | Prep Time: 5 mins | Cooking Time: 0

Ingredients

- 2 cups fish bone broth
- 2 teaspoons Herbs de Provence
- 1 teaspoon fresh mint leaves
- Pinch of black pepper
- 1 tablespoon ghee
- Salt to taste

Directions

1. Place the Herbs de Provence in a small sachet.
2. Set a small fire and heat the bone broth until it begins to bubble.
3. Add the herbs and simmer for 15-20 minutes until they start to release their flavors. Meanwhile, pray to whichever gods you believe in that it works. A little divine intervention can't hurt.
4. Take the plants out of the broth, and add the ghee, salt, and pepper.
5. Stir and finish with the crushed mint leaves for a refreshing drink. And pray again.

Prepare the drink every day because it is packed with collagen and will keep your skin looking young and plump.

Sound of Walder Frey heavy breathing

"WHAT DO WE SAY TO VEGANISM? NOT TODAY!"

IV. OF BEAST AND BIRD

Enjoy these fine meat and poultry feasts complete with your favorite bone broths and stocks to keep your sword arm strong and your mind sharp.

LANNISTER HOT POT

Tyrion Lannister's diminutive stature made him a source of constant ridicule, even among his own family. Jaime was his only ally, and determined to put hair on his little brother's chest and help the "half-man" become whole, he concocted this spicy roast recipe for courage and strength.

Serves: 4-6 | Prep Time: 10 mins | Cooking Time: 4-6 hours

Ingredients

- 1 ¾ pounds beef roast
- 2 ½ cups bone broth (from something you made before, or create something new)
- 2 tablespoons butter
- ½ cup water
- 2 garlic cloves
- 1 cup frozen cranberries
- 1 teaspoon horseradish powder
- 1 teaspoon ginger powder
- 1 cinnamon stick
- 6 cloves
- ¼ cup honey
- Salt and pepper to taste

Directions

1. Rub the meat with the salt and pepper.

2. Take a large cauldron, place it over a fire, and add the butter.

3. Let it melt and place the meat inside.

4. Roast on all sides until slightly brown. It should take about 10 minutes. Take out of the cauldron and set aside afterwards.

5. Add ½ cup bone broth and scrape out all the meat bits that get stuck to the pot walls. Don't leave them behind; they are very tasty!

6. Let the meat bathe in the broth for 5-6 minutes.

7. Stir in the water, spices, garlic, cranberries, and honey. Let cook for about 5 minutes.

8. Put the meat back in the pot, and stir until coated with the cranberry sauce.

9. Pour in the remaining broth and simmer for 4-6 hours, checking from time to time to see if it needs more water.

10. Place the meat on a large slab of wood and spoon the sauce over it.

Keep the roast in the fridge for a maximum of 2-3 days if you don't manage to finish it right away.

Though Tyrion may never have grown as tall as his big brother, he certainly had the biggest cajones of the two, as he demonstrated by slapping his nephew in one of the most historic moments of all time. Come on, we've all wanted to do it.

REJUVENATING RED MEAT

Lady Melisandre was hot enough to turn even the erstwhile severe and rigid Stannis into a pathetic pool of male hormones.

But as anybody who has ever used a makeup wipe will know, not everything is always as it seems. In the comfort of her own home, The Red Woman removed her necklace and jumped into her PJs, allowing us all to see her as she really was.

So long as you dine on hearty bone broth dishes such as this, you too will enjoy the mirage of eternal youth.

Serves: 4 | Prep Time: 30 mins | Cooking Time: 15 mins

Ingredients

- 1 pound flank steak
- ¼ cup beef bone broth
- ¼ teaspoon fish sauce
- 2 tablespoons coconut oil
- 1 head broccoli, chopped into florets
- 1 ½ tablespoons sesame oil
- 2 garlic cloves
- 2 scallions
- 1 small piece grated ginger
- 5 tablespoons coconut aminos
- 1 teaspoon arrowroot powder
- Sesame oil

Directions

1. Melisandre preferred tender and juicy meat, so the first step is to prepare a marinade from 1 tablespoon sesame oil, 1 chopped scallion, 1 crushed garlic clove, ginger, and fish sauce.

2. Coat the beef with this marinade and let it rest for about half an hour.

3. Take a separate bowl and mix the broth with ½ teaspoon sesame oil, arrowroot powder, and the remaining garlic clove.

4. Set a fire and place a skillet on top of it. This shouldn't be a problem for a Red Priestess.

5. Put the coconut oil in the pan, and wait for it to heat through. You can observe the omens while you wait.

6. Add the meat, and cook for 2 minutes on each side until slightly brown.

7. Take it out of the skillet and set aside for now.

8. Next, add the broccoli florets to the skillet and roast for about 2 minutes.

9. Pour over 1-2 tablespoons of water, and place a lid on. Let it cook this way for a couple of minutes.

10. Remove the lid and keep cooking until you like how the broccoli looks and you are eager to eat it.

11. Bring the meat back to the pan, add the arrowroot powder sauce, and stir well.

12. Cook until just warm.

13. Serve with your preferred side dish.

You should only cook what you plan to eat for your meal. The beef can be kept in the fridge for the next day, but the broccoli will lose its texture and become limp.

Be sure to use your newfound powers responsibly.

HUMBLE PIE

All of King's Landing gathered to throw groceries at Cersei as she took a humbling naked walk through the streets. As always, the queen mother would have the last laugh, though, as upon reaching the Red Keep she had collected all the ingredients required for a fine supper, saving her a trip to the markets. Win.

If you prefer to do your grocery shopping in a more conventional and much less humiliating manner, here's what you'll be needing.

Serves: 6 | Prep Time: 10 mins | Cooking Time: 1 ½ hours

Ingredients

- 2 pounds ground beef
- 1 large onion, diced
- 1 cup frozen peas, thawed
- 4 medium carrots, diced
- 1 cup green beans, sliced
- 2 tablespoons ghee
- 1 cup beef bone broth
- 2 teaspoons dried rosemary
- ½ teaspoon ground black pepper
- 2 teaspoons dried thyme
- Small bunch of fresh parsley
- 6 gold potatoes, peeled and quartered
- 3 tablespoons arrowroot powder
- 1 ½ teaspoons salt

Directions

1. Being high-born, you probably have a great oven in your keep. Preheat it to 350°F.

2. Place the potatoes into a small pot and cover with water. Add some salt, and wait until it starts to bubble. The potatoes should be cooked through in about 20 minutes. They will be ready when you can easily perforate them with a fork.

3. Transfer to a sieve to discard any liquid.

4. Add 1 tablespoon ghee and crush the potatoes until they are smooth.

5. Heat the remaining quantity of ghee in a skillet over a fire and sauté the onion for 5 minutes.

6. Add the meat, and cook until you no longer see anything pink in the pan.

7. Add the veggies and cook them for about 5 minutes.

8. Stir in the rosemary, thyme, chopped parsley, and arrowroot powder.

9. Pour over the broth and cook, stirring continuously until the sauce thickens.

10. Remove from the fire, and season with salt and pepper.

11. Transfer the skillet's content into a baking dish.

12. Cover with the mashed potatoes, and bake for about 50 minutes until slightly brown on the edges. The queen found it difficult to wait, but the result was worth it.

13. Let it cool a little and serve.

You may keep what's left of the pie in the fridge for the next day, or freeze it for later. But this outcome highly unlikely; you won't be able to keep your hands off it.

THREE-EYED STIR-FRY

Ever fallen into a "food coma" after a heavy meal? Bran Stark takes that to a whole new level.

The Three-Eyed Raven passed the knowledge of this recipe onto his young apprentice, who gobbled it up so voraciously that he fell into a deep vision state.

This is how he learned Hodor's real name, Wylis, and all about his aunt, Lyanna. So if your family is harboring secrets, just knock up this hearty lamb and veg stir-fry and all will be revealed.

Serves: 3-4 | Prep Time: 5 mins | Cooking Time: 30 minutes

Ingredients

- 2 cup lamb meat, cut into chunks
- 2 tablespoons coconut oil
- 1 cup beef bone broth
- 3 cup chopped vegetables (a combination of carrots, peas, and broccoli)
- ¼ cup honey
- Small handful of fresh cilantro
- 1 tablespoon cumin seeds
- Salt and pepper to taste

Directions

1. Place 1 tablespoon of coconut oil into a pot and heat it over a small fire.

2. Bring in the meat chunks and cook until brown on all sides.

3. Remove the meat and let it rest for a while.

4. Next, add the remaining oil, and when it's hot, add the cumin seeds. Cook for about 2 minutes.

5. Add the veggies, and bring them to the desired degree of doneness.

6. Place the meat back in.

7. Pour in the broth, and add the honey. Stir with a large animal bone or spoon.

8. Cook over a low flame until the liquid decreases and thickens.

9. Sprinkle some salt and pepper, and serve with your best side dish.

In the unlikely even that you don't finish every last morsel, this stir-fry can be kept in the fridge for the next day.

Whenever there were leftovers, Summer, Bran's direwolf, took care of them and could be seen twitching in delight while dreaming of chasing rabbits.

PIOUS PORK CHOPS

The High Sparrow was a man beyond all forms of earthly temptation, except one: he loved pork chop night more than Homer Simpson.

He roped in his entire clergy to help with the weekly preparations, because as we know, the people always do the dirty work.

Be sure to say grace before you tuck into this tasty treat.

Serves: 4 | Prep Time: 15 mins | Cooking Time: 17 mins

Ingredients

- 4 pork chops
- 1 pear, sliced
- 2 shallots
- 2 pitted dates
- ¾ cup pork broth
- 3 tablespoons apple cider vinegar
- 1 tablespoon coconut oil
- Pinch of cayenne
- Salt and pepper to taste
- Small bunch of cilantro leaves

Directions

1. Preheat your modest oven to 350°F.
2. Place a metal baking sheet inside so it gets hot.
3. Rub the chops with salt and pepper.
4. Take a skillet, and heat the coconut oil over a small fire you made yourself.
5. Slightly brown the meat. It should be nearly done in 8 minutes.
6. Remove from the skillet and place on a baking sheet. Bake for about 10 minutes. Meanwhile, simply meditate on life's meaning.
7. While the pork is in the oven, prepare the sweet and spicy sauce.
8. Use the skillet to sauté the shallots for approximately 2 minutes.
9. Add the pear slices and cook for 2 minutes more.
10. Stir in the vinegar, dates, cayenne, and broth. Cook until you get a thick sauce.
11. Arrange the chops on a huge plate, and coat with the pear sauce.
12. Top with chopped parsley and enjoy.

If you can't eat all this food at a single sitting, that's okay, just keep it in the fridge and enjoy the next day.

One last word of advice: you'll want to use an electric oven for this recipe, and not wildfire.

BEAR'S BEEF STEW

People believe Jaime Lannister to be a villain, a man without honor; however, he must have some good in him somewhere. Otherwise, why would he jump into the bear pit to save Brienne?

Jaime's actions could have gotten them both killed. Luckily, Lord Bolton's men were eager to gain favor - and gold - from Tywin, so they plucked the two out safe and sound. In addition, they served them with a delicious stew.

If you have a feast to throw, or some serious butt kissing to do, this recipe is a surefire winner.

Serves: 12 | Prep Time: 10 mins | Cooking Time: 8 hours 30 mins

Ingredients

- 3 pounds beef stew meat, chopped into small pieces
- 4 cups beef bone broth
- 10 oz. mushrooms
- 2 tablespoons olive oil
- 1 ½ pounds potatoes, diced
- 2 tablespoons taco seasoning
- 4 tablespoons butter
- 2 teaspoons salt
- 5 tablespoons arrowroot powder
- 1 ½ cups diced onion
- 1 cup frozen peas
- 6-8 garlic cloves, chopped
- 1 teaspoon dried thyme
- ¼ teaspoon allspice
- 1 teaspoon dried basil
- 1 teaspoon dried oregano
- 1 ½ cups carrots, diced
- 3 tablespoons tomato paste
- Handful of fresh parsley, chopped
- Lard for cooking
- Salt and pepper to taste

Directions

1. Put stew meat in a bowl, and add the olive oil, pepper, salt, and seasoning.

2. Take a little bit of lard, and heat it in a large skillet. Compliment Jamie on his impeccable hair.

3. Cook the beef until brown. Work in batches if you need to.

4. Those Bolton boys always carried a crockpot with them (just in case), so use your own for this recipe. Throw the mushrooms, tomato paste, broth, arrowroot, butter, spices, herbs and meat in the slow cooker.

5. Cook for 60 minutes on high.

6. Bring in the carrots, potatoes and pearl onions and let it cook for another 7 hours.

7. Finally, bring the peas to the pot.

8. Cover with chopped parsley and serve.

Keep this stew for up to 3 days in the fridge, and halve the quantities if you feel that this is too much for you.

Of course, the poor old bear never did get to eat that day, so he would surely welcome your leftovers.

RAMSAY'S BEEF CHILI

Everyone has that one friend who takes practical jokes too far. Ramsay Bolton is that guy. Or was that guy. When he wasn't flaying people for a laugh, he was watching them try to knock back his hot beef chili with a straight face.

It is not advisable to carry out this prank on redheads. They have been known to hold a grudge.

Serves: 6-8 | Prep Time: 10 mins | Cooking Time: 8 hours 15 mins

Ingredients

- 2 pounds beef stew meat, cut into small pieces
- 12 oz. bacon, crispy cooked, chopped
- 3-4 jalapeños, diced
- 2 onions, chopped
- 2 bell peppers (any color), chopped
- 1 cup bone broth
- 2 cups diced celery
- 8-9 garlic cloves, chopped
- 4 cups crushed tomatoes
- 2 teaspoons chili powder
- ½ teaspoon cayenne pepper
- 4 tablespoons butter
- 1 teaspoon dried thyme
- ¼ teaspoon cinnamon
- 2 teaspoons cumin seeds
- ½ teaspoon turmeric powder
- 3 tablespoons maple syrup
- 2 teaspoons dried oregano
- Salt to taste

Directions

1. Coat the meat with salt.

2. Heat 1 tablespoon of butter.

3. Take the meat and cook until brown. Work in batches if you don't have such a large skillet.

4. Throw the beef in the crockpot.

5. Add 2 tablespoons of butter to the pan, and sauté the onion and garlic for 6-7 minutes. Bring them to the crockpot.

6. Throw all the other ingredients into the pot and stir well.

7. Cook on low for 7-8 hours.

8. Serve while it's still warm.

The chili can be kept in the fridge for up to 2 days. The leftovers are absolutely not suitable for dogs.

Oh, and if Ramsay Bolton ever offers you a pork sausage, just get the hell out of there.

HOMECOMING CHICKEN PIE

When Sansa Stark finally managed to escape Winterfell and her psychopathic husband, she and Theon were caught by Ramsay's men, and were nearly torn apart by his dogs.

Fortunately, Brienne of Tarth appeared like a knight in not-so-shining armor and saved the redhead and her unfortunate companion. Nothing warms the soul like a hearty chicken pie, so to finally earn Sansa's trust Brienne had Podrick rustle up this recipe.

Serves: 6 | Prep Time: 20 mins | Cooking Time: 45 mins

Ingredients

- 2 cups chopped chicken breast, no bones
- 16 oz. mixed veggies, frozen
- 1 ½ cups chicken bone broth
- 1 cup homemade cream of mushroom soup
- 1 teaspoon dried thyme
- Small bunch of dill, chopped
- 1 teaspoon dried thyme
- Salt and pepper to taste

For the crust:

- 1 cup flour
- ½ cup melted butter
- 1 ½ teaspoons baking powder
- 1 cup milk
- ¼ teaspoon salt

Directions

1. In a large dish, combine all the ingredients, except the ones for the crust, and stir well.

2. Place the mixture in a baking dish. Podrick, ever ready for any situation and keen to please, had an entire arsenal of crockery in his saddlebags.

3. Combine the ingredients for the crust.

4. Pour the batter over the meat mixture.

5. Heat the oven to 375°F and bake for 45-50 minutes.

Keep the pie in the fridge if you have some left. Difficult to believe you will, though.

There you have it, the perfect recipe to impress a future ruler. Or just your Instagram followers, which is important too.

FRIENDZONE CASSEROLE

Jorah had finally plucked up the courage to declare his feelings for Daenerys. He had the meal set, the candles burning, and all that stood between him and the love of his life was a gentle stroll through Astapor while the final preparations were made in their absence.

Daenerys was delighted when a little girl engaged her in a playful game. Curious, Dany grabbed the girl's toy, but before she could open it a cloaked figure shoved her aside and skewered a deadly manticore with his blade before it could attack.

By way of gratitude, Dany insisted that the hero of the hour - none other than Barristan Selmy - accompany them home for dinner, despite Jorah's protestations that three is a crowd. It was thus that Mormont was well and truly friendzoned.

Serves: 6 | Prep Time: 10 mins | Cooking Time: 75 mins

Ingredients

- 2 cups pre-cooked chicken
- 1 pound frozen broccoli
- ¼ cup melted butter
- ¾ cup bone broth
- 2 cups shredded cheese
- ½ cup long grain rice
- 5 garlic cloves
- 3 celery stalks, chopped
- 1 teaspoon dried thyme
- 1 teaspoon dried basil
- 2 cans condensed cream of chicken soup
- 3 carrots, chopped
- 1 onion, diced
- Salt and pepper to taste

Directions

1. Take a large skillet from your kitchen and heat the butter.
2. Add the celery, onion, and carrot, and season with salt, pepper, and herbs. Cook for 8-10 minutes.
3. Stir in the garlic and cook for 1 more minute.
4. Combine the veggies with all the other ingredients in a large bowl.
5. Stir well and transfer all the vegetables to a greased baking dish.
6. Heat the oven to 375°F and bake the casserole for about 60 minutes. Try not to leave Jorah and Barristan alone; it could be awkward.

If you don't need the food right that moment, you may skip the baking part and keep it in the fridge for later.

And let this be a lesson to you all: leave nothing unimportant unsaid, for you never know when another player will come along!

BENJEN'S CHICKEN & BACON BREAKFAST

Bran had thought his uncle long gone, but when a mysterious hooded savior rescued the Stark boy from encroaching walkers, it was revealed to be Benjen.

When you're trapped north of the wall without your pals, don't have much in the stores and need to get back to work quickly, try this recipe for breakfast or lunch.

If you need help hunting down the chicken, it does help to have a Warg on hand.

Serves: 4 | Prep Time: 5 mins | Cooking Time: 20 mins

Ingredients

- 1 cup cooked chicken, chopped
- ½ cup chicken bone broth
- 1 sweet potato, chopped
- 4 bacon strips
- 1 box frozen spinach
- 2 garlic cloves, minced
- ½ onion, diced
- Salt and pepper to taste

Directions

1. Roast the bacon in a large skillet until crispy.
2. Remove and set aside on a plate.
3. Add the chicken, and cook a little bit in the fat remaining from the bacon.
4. Add the onion and sweet potato. Sauté for about 10 minutes.
5. Stir in the garlic and cook for 1 more minute.
6. Add the spinach, and pour the broth. Cook until the spinach wilts and the liquid evaporates.
7. Serve with bacon strips on top for your favorite nephew.

In case you want to keep this dish in the fridge, skip the bacon part. When it comes into contact with cold, bacon becomes greasy.

If you don't have a Warg on hand to help with the hunting, some say that the male of the species can be trained to head out to the supermarket and find their own way back.

VALHAR MEATBALLIS

All men must dine. And there are few dishes more satisfying than this Braavosi special, a firm favorite of Jaqen H'ghar.

If the day comes when you wish to try this recipe for yourself, just give your coin to any man from Braavos and say these words to him: "valar meatballis."

Serves: 6-8 | Prep Time: 15 mins | Cooking Time: 40 mins

Ingredients

- 1 pound ground pork
- 1 cup chicken bone broth
- 1 egg
- 4 tablespoons tomato puree
- ½ teaspoon dried oregano
- Small bunch of dill
- Small bunch of parsley
- Salt and pepper to taste
- 4 tablespoons ghee

Directions

1. Combine the meat, greens, and oregano.
2. Break the egg, and stir it in.
3. Shape into several meatballs.
4. Set up a fire and heat 2 tablespoons of ghee in a large skillet.
5. Cook the meatballs until brown on all sides.
6. Add the tomato puree, and season with salt and pepper.
7. Pour in half of the stock and stir well.
8. Let cook over a low flame until the sauce thickens.
9. Keep adding broth until you reach the desired consistency.
10. Serve with mashed potatoes, rice, or whatever side dish you prefer.

Place the meatballs in the fridge and keep them there for up to 3 days, or freeze for later. Stick 'em with the pointy end, and enjoy!

PETYR'S CHICKEN PATTIES

Lysa Arryn took protective parenting to the next level. She insisted on a gluten and sugar free diet for her young son. Unfortunately, social services were unable to convince her to adopt a dairy free approach too.

Petyr "Littlefinger" Baelish was so disgusted with his new wife that he accidentally on purpose pushed her through the Moon Door.

Since then, young Robin has been growing strong thanks to this patty recipe, among others, introduced by his new guardian.

Serves: 4 | Prep Time: 10 mins | Cooking Time: 15 mins

Ingredients

- 1 pound ground chicken
- 2 tablespoons maple syrup
- 2 tablespoons ghee
- 2 garlic cloves, minced
- 1 medium apple, diced
- 3-4 tablespoons bone broth
- Small handful of parsley leaves
- Lard for cooking
- Sausage seasoning to taste

Directions

1. Combine the meat, garlic, parsley leaves, apple, and maple syrup in a large bowl. Mix with care, like a loving mother.

2. Shape the mixture into small patties.

3. Melt the lard in a large skillet.

4. Cook the patties on both sides until cooked through. This should take about 12-15 minutes. They should be just perfect: not too charred and not too soft—otherwise, Robin might get all bratty about it.

5. When you flip them over, add a tablespoon of bone broth at a time, so they don't get burnt.

6. Serve with mashed potatoes or brown rice.

You can keep the patties in the fridge for up to 3 days, or in the freezer if you want to use them later.

You can keep Robin as long as you want. Nobody else wants him.

V. FROM LAND AND SEA

Hearty meals of fish and vegetables have raised some of the most formidable warriors in all the Seven Kingdoms. Try them and see for yourself.

IRON ISLANDS HALIBUT

When two women make an alliance, people should prepare for interesting times. And so it is with the pact between Yara Greyjoy and Daenerys Targaryen, which promises to bring havoc to the Seven Kingdoms.

As if Theon couldn't feel any more emasculated, he was sent to the kitchens by his little sister to prepare a celebratory feast to toast the new alliance. He prepared this Iron Islands specialty, and may well have found his calling as a cook.

Serves: 4 | Prep Time: 10 mins | Cooking Time: 20 mins

Ingredients

- 1 ½ pounds halibut fillets
- 4 cups chicken bone broth
- 4 scallions
- 1 lemongrass stalk, chopped
- 1 tablespoon fish sauce
- 1 small piece fresh ginger, grated
- ¼ cup coconut milk
- 1 tablespoon soy sauce
- 4 garlic cloves, minced

Directions

1. Take a large saucepan and add the broth, garlic, lemongrass, ginger, and soy and fish sauces. Use quality ingredients, like the ones Yara brought from home.

2. Add the fish, and toss to coat.

3. Heat the whole mixture until the broth starts to bubble. Flirt outrageously.

4. Set the fire on low and cook for 15 minutes, but do not let the sauce boil.

5. Pour in the coconut milk and add the scallions.

6. Cook for another 5 minutes.

7. Serve hot.

Prepare only the amount you need for a meal because you cannot keep the fish in the fridge for later.

This recipe once belonged to Balon Greyjoy. In fact, he loved fish so much that now he's sleeping with them.

DRAGONS' TILAPIA TREAT

Feeding dragons is no easy thing, and expensive enough to bankrupt a kingdom before it even gets going. Thankfully Daenerys could rely on a plentiful source of fish in Mereen.

During the second siege she kept her babies well fed on this simple soup. They gobbled it up so voraciously that they each experienced mild heartburn afterwards, which was most unfortunate for the Masters' fleet.

Serves: 4 | Prep Time: 10 mins | Cooking Time: 30 mins

Ingredients

- 1 pound tilapia fillets (from Mereen's fish market)
- 4 cups chicken bone broth
- 1 cup jasmine rice
- 4 cups arugula leaves, torn
- 2 cups water
- ¼ cup fresh mint, chopped
- Zest and juice of 1 lime
- 2 scallions, chopped
- 1 cup carrots, shredded
- Small bunch of cilantro leaves

Directions

1. Add the water to a pot, and add the rice.

2. Place over a fire. Cook for about 20 minutes, until all the water is gone.

3. Add the lime zest and juice and stir well.

4. Take another pot and pour in the broth.

5. When it starts to slightly bubble, bring in the fish and cook for around 5 minutes.

6. Take it off and break into small pieces.

7. To serve: place a portion of rice into a large bowl. Add fish, carrot, arugula, scallions, and mint. Top with chopped cilantro leaves.

Only cook the fish you need for one meal, and prepare the veggies and herbs on the spot so that they are fresh and don't oxidize.

And be sure to savor the taste. You don't want to gulp it down so fast that you end up belching and burning down the neighbor's fence.

SELYSE'S SPICY LEMON HADDOCK

Selyse Baratheon was a melancholy woman on the brink of madness whose husband, Stannis, had placed her aside to take up with a woman he'd found on Tinder. Yes, that's a tenuous fire joke.

Selyse, remembering that the key to every man's heart is through his stomach, decided to prepare an exquisite dinner for her estranged husband, adding a little zest and spice to the dish in the hope that it would have a knock-on effect in the bedroom.

Serves: 4-6 | Prep Time: 15 mins | Cooking Time: 40 mins

Ingredients

- 4 haddock fillets, boneless
- 4 cups celery, chopped
- 2 tablespoons olive oil
- 1 cup onion, chopped
- 3 cups chicken bone broth
- 2 cups bell peppers, chopped
- ½ cup tomato paste
- 1 tablespoon lemon zest
- 2 tablespoons lemon juice
- 1 tablespoon hot chili powder

Directions

1. Preheat the oven to 375°F.
2. Take a large oven dish with a lid, and pour in the olive oil.
3. Place all the veggies inside.
4. Pour in the broth, and add the tomato paste. Stir well.
5. Add the lemon juice and zest, and chili powder.
6. Lock the lid on and bake for 20 minutes. Make sure everything is as it should be. You know Stannis will take any opportunity to complain.
7. Add the fish fillets on top of the veggies.
8. Cook for 20 minutes, flipping over after 10 minutes.
9. Selyse served the fillets with brown rice and a glass of white wine.

Only prepare the quantity you need because, if all goes well, you'll be whisked off your feet before you can even think about packing up.

When asked for his thoughts on the sumptuous feast, Stannis remarked:

"Hmm, it was alright."

High praise indeed.

BONE-SETTING SOUP

Despite being a dog, Sandor Clegane seems to have the nine lives of a cat. After Brienne kicked his sorry butt, everybody assumed he was gone for. As it happens, he was rescued by some peaceful folk who fed him with this bone-setting fish soup.

This recipe helped nurse The Hound back to full health, just in time to give The Brotherhood Without Banners a good hiding.

Serves: 4 | Prep Time: 25 mins | Cooking Time: 35 mins

Ingredients

- 1 pound cod fillets, cut into cubes
- 3 ½ cups chicken bone broth
- ¼ cup onion, chopped
- 1 tablespoon butter
- 1 cup frozen green beans
- 1 cup carrots, sliced
- ½ cup frozen corn
- 1 garlic clove, chopped
- ½ teaspoon dried basil
- 1 teaspoon peppercorns
- 1 bay leaf
- ½ teaspoon dried oregano
- Salt and pepper to taste

Directions

1. Take a large pot and melt the butter inside.

2. Place the garlic and onion inside, and sauté for a couple of minutes.

3. Add all the other ingredients, except for the fish.

4. When the broth starts to bubble, lower the flame and cook for about 8 minutes. Meanwhile, why not talk to your neighbors; ask how their day has been, learn about the movements of your enemies, and what day the bins are emptied around here.

5. Stir in the fish and cook for 6-7 minutes more.

6. Serve surrounded with dear friends.

If, by any chance, you don't finish the whole pot of soup, just place it in the fridge and enjoy the next day.

The healing properties of this dish will have you fighting fit in no time. So put on your new boots, pick up your axe and get out there!

OLENNA'S VEG RISOTTO

Lady Olenna Tyrell spent most of her time in King's Landing walking through the gardens of the Red Keep, where she would occasionally swoop down and pull up plump, ripe vegetables, stowing them under her considerable garb and smuggling them back home.

Olenna's predominantly vegetarian diet, complemented by bone broth, have allowed The Queen of Thorns to stay sharp even in old age, which is useful when you've got to deal with a little pr!ck like Joffrey.

Serves: 4 | Prep Time: 5 mins | Cooking Time: 30 mins

Ingredients

- ½ cup uncooked quinoa (soaked overnight)
- 1 cup butternut squash puree
- 1 ½ cups chicken bone broth
- 1 tablespoon coconut oil
- Salt and pepper to taste
- 2 tablespoons grated parmesan

Directions

1. Place the quinoa, together with 1 cup bone broth, in a small pot and bring to a boil. Cook for about 15-20 minutes. Remove from the flame.
2. Fluff with a fork, and add the purée, coconut oil and remaining broth. Stir well.
3. Return the quinoa to the fire, and cook for 12-15 minutes.
4. Season to taste and serve topped with grated parmesan.

You may cook only the quinoa and place it in the fridge for later when you have time to prepare delicious food with it.

And please, get your groceries from the store; you don't want to start a war with the neighbors.

SAM'S SWEET POTATO

Samwell Tarly knew how to do precisely two things: read and eat. When he arrived at Castle Black, he found neither of those skills was particularly valuable to the men of the Night's Watch.

Jon Snow, all-round nice guy, took Tarly under his wing and committed to helping his friend slim down and toughen up. This simple recipe fuelled Sam through his vigorous training sessions. Yes, unfortunately you still have to do those.

Serves: 10 | Prep Time: 15 mins | Cooking Time: 4 hours

Ingredients

- 2 cooked sweet potatoes, chopped
- 1 cup chicken bone broth
- 1 cup celery, chopped
- 6 cups dry bread crumbs
- 1 cup onion, chopped
- ½ cup walnuts, chopped
- ½ cup butter
- Salt and pepper to taste

Directions

1. Take a saucepan, place it on a fire, and melt the butter.
2. Sauté the celery and onion for 6-8 minutes.
3. Pour in the broth, and season with salt and pepper.
4. Throw in all the remaining ingredients and stir well.
5. Transfer the contents to a crockpot, and cook on low for 4 hours.

Keep in the fridge to enjoy later. This little number will remain delicious even after 3 days.

Tarly ended up ditching his Castle Black gym membership and went back to reading, but he never tired of this recipe.

BRONN'S BAKED FENNEL

Bronn is a skilled warrior, and he has a very special relationship with Tyrion Lannister that people nowadays might call a "bromance."

Their colorful conversations are legendary and the two quickly became dependent on each other: the mercenary requiring Tyrion's money, the imp Bronn's sword.

However, not for all the money in the world would Bronn agree to fight The Mountain for Tyrion. But the little Lannister couldn't hold a grudge against his friend: he knew how fierce a fighter Ser Gregor Clegane was.

He preferred to remember the fun they had together, eating good food and drinking excellent wine. They had one favorite dish, and Bronn managed to smuggle some in before parting ways with his friend.

Serves: 4 | Prep Time: 10 mins | Cooking Time: 1 hour

Ingredients

- 1 medium fennel bulb
- ¼ cup coconut milk
- 1 ½ pounds potatoes
- ¼ cup chicken bone broth
- Small bunch of dill, chopped
- Salt and pepper to taste
- A dash of devilish wit

Directions

1. Preheat your oven to 400°F.

2. Slightly grease a small baking dish with cooking fat.

3. Take a sharp knife and slice the potatoes and fennel. Do you know that fennel goes well with wine?

4. Place the layers in the dish like this: ⅓ of the potatoes, half of the fennel slices, some salt and pepper and a sprinkling of half the dill; another ⅓ potatoes, the rest of the fennel, dill, salt and pepper again; the remaining potatoes and perhaps some more salt and pepper.

5. Add the broth and coconut milk.

6. They should be cooked through in about one hour.

Keep in the fridge for the next day if you are so fed up that you cannot eat the whole thing.

Tyrion and Bronn remained good friends until the former departed in unceremonious circumstances. Perhaps they shall meet again.

UNBURNT KALE

Never invite Daenerys Targaryen to a barbeque. The men of Vaes Dothrak discovered this to their cost when she pulled out her "watch me burn your house down and walk out alive" party trick.

Since this incident, it has been deemed wise to try to serve the Khaleesi vegetable based dishes wherever possible.

Serves: 2 | Prep Time: 10 mins | Cooking Time: 15 mins

Ingredients

- 2 bunches of kale, rinsed, stems removed and torn
- ½ cup beef bone broth
- 3 tablespoons butter
- Salt and pepper to taste

Directions

1. Take a large pan, and place it on a fire set by one of your many attendants. Distract Khaleesi with something shiny.
2. Place 2 tablespoons of butter in the pan.
3. After it melts, pour the broth, and then add the kale.
4. Cook for about 5 minutes, stirring, until the greens wilt. Don't cook it any longer if you want it to keep the incombustible properties.
5. Remove from the fire, and place a lid on the pan. Let it rest for 6-7 minutes.
6. Season to taste, add another tablespoon of butter, and enjoy with anything you want.

It would be best to cook only the amount you need for a meal, to ensure it is as fresh as can be.

If you cook the kale just right, Dany might just forget all about her party trick, and your hut will be safe for another day.

"EVERYTHING'S BETTER WITH SOME BROTH IN THE BELLY."

VI. SWEET THINGS

No feast is complete without a decadent dessert. These treats are fit for warriors, kings and queens alike, thanks to a very special ingredient.

TYWIN'S MUFFINS

Unfortunately for Tyrion, his father never showed him much affection. He considered his son responsible for his wife's death, and wanted nothing more than to be rid of the imp.

In one final attempt to gain his daddy's approval, Tyrion put his heart and soul into a peace offering of delicious muffins. It was a beautiful, loving gesture. He trawled through every dusty cookbook and eventually came across this recipe featuring bone broth protein powder.

You can pick up some of that good stuff here: http://geni.us/bonebrothpowder

Serves: 15 muffins | Prep Time: 5 mins | Cooking Time: 12 mins

Ingredients

- ¾ cup whole wheat flour
- 1 very ripe banana
- 2 scoops bone broth protein powder
- ¾ cup filled with egg whites
- ½ cup Greek yogurt
- 1 teaspoon baking powder
- 1 teaspoon baking soda
- ½ teaspoon cinnamon

Directions

1. Preheat your oven to 350°F.
2. Use a food processor to mix all the ingredients.
3. Lightly grease a muffin tin.
4. Spoon the batter into each muffin case, filling about ¾ of their height. You may even use a wine cup to do it.
5. Bake for about 12 minutes or until a wooden skewer comes out clean.

If you keep them in a dry and dark place, like Tywin's mind, they will last up to 3 days.

Try not to overreact if your father doesn't take to the muffins immediately.

DANY'S BLUEBERRY SWEET BREAD

Just like any woman who wants to make an impression on a charming man, Dany wanted to cook for Daario Naharis. And nothing is more romantic for a meathead than a dessert using bone broth protein powder, right?

The Mother of Dragons knocked this recipe up in just 40 minutes, and in return Daario brought her a bag full of her enemy's heads. Awww.

Serves: 8 | Prep Time: 5 mins | Cooking Time: 35 mins

Ingredients

- ½ cup oat flour
- ¼ cup almond meal
- 1 egg
- 1 scoop bone broth protein powder
- ¼ cup cream cheese
- ½ cup blueberries
- ¼ cup brown sugar
- 3 tablespoons milk

Directions

1. Preheat the oven to 350°F.
2. Take a loaf pan and line it with parchment paper. If you have some pink paper, even better.
3. In a bowl, mix together the wet ingredients (egg, milk, cream cheese) until soft.
4. Stir in the remaining ingredients.
5. Pour the mixture you've just prepared with great love into the loaf pan and bake for about 35 minutes.
6. Serve and enjoy!

Keep it in a dry place for one day. After that, you might need to place it in the fridge.

TYRION'S TRUSTY TRUFFLES

As Tyrion prepared to meet Daenerys, the scheming Lannister knew he couldn't present himself to the Khaleesi with bare hands if he wanted to gain her trust.

He settled upon a gift known to have brought truces to even the bitterest of enemies. These decadent dark chocolate truffles are irresistible, and form a powerful bond between the recipient and the giver.

Serves: 8 | Prep Time: 15 mins | Cooking Time: 5 mins

Ingredients

- ¼ cup almond milk
- ¼ cup dates, pitted and chopped
- ⅛ cup oats
- ¼ cup coconut oil
- ¼ cup bone broth protein powder
- 1 tablespoon coconut flour
- 2 tablespoons honey
- 2 dark chocolate bars

Directions

1. Mix the dates, almond milk, protein powder, oats, honey, and coconut flour with care.
2. Shape into eight small balls.
3. Take a saucepan, and let the coconut oil melt together with the chocolate over very low heat.
4. Remove from the flame, and let cool a little bit.
5. Use tongs to soak each ball in the chocolate sauce.
6. Place in the freezer for the exterior layer to harden.

You don't seriously think that there will be anything left, do you? If you somehow manage to resist temptation, just keep them in the fridge.

Dany was so delighted with Tyrion's truffles that she named him Hand of the Queen. So, if you're looking for that big promotion, rustle up these trusty truffles for your boss and watch the magic happen.

RESURRECTION POUND CAKE

Jon Snow was dead, and that was not a good thing for any of the residents of the Seven Kingdoms. Although some of them (for example the ones who killed him) seemed to think it was a great idea to get rid of the Lord Commander, Ser Davos knew that he had to do whatever he could to bring Jon back to life.

He asked Melisandre to do the job. Even if he hated the Red Priestess, Ser Davos knew that she was the only one that could perform a feat like this. She prepared this pound cake and left it to work its magic.

Serves: 4 | Prep Time: 5 mins | Cooking Time: 35 mins

Ingredients

- ½ cup egg whites
- 4 drops stevia
- 1 cup bone broth protein powder
- ½ cup egg whites
- 1 teaspoon vanilla extract
- ½ cup steamed cauliflower
- 2 eggs
- ¼ teaspoon cinnamon
- Pinch of salt

Directions

1. Preheat your oven to 325°F.
2. Put all the ingredients into a food processor, and mix until you get a smooth batter. Or, if you are a tough man, use a whisk to do it.
3. Pour the batter into a small loaf pan.
4. Bake for approximately 35 minutes until slightly brown on top.

Keep the remaining cake in a dry place for 24 hours or in the fridge for up to 3 days. Jon should keep for at least that long.

If you too have been violently murdered by your colleagues, or just had a particularly strenuous leg day, this will work wonders.

WAFFLES FOR SERIOUS PEOPLE

Tyrion Lannister was a man of many words and loved nothing more than to exercise hit wit among good company. Imagine his horror, then, when his jest fell completely flat with Grey Worm and Missandei.

He offered them wine, and they refused. He told them jokes, and they stared blankly back at him. Thankfully, he was hit by a brilliant idea: waffles. Because it is literally impossible to be serious when you have waffles sitting in front of you. Go ahead and try it for yourself.

Serves: 8 | Prep Time: 5 mins | Cooking Time: 30 mins

Ingredients

- 2 scoops bone broth protein powder
- ¼ cup cottage cheese
- 1 cup almond meal
- 2 eggs
- ⅓ cup almond milk
- 1 teaspoon cinnamon
- 1 tablespoon coconut oil
- 1 teaspoon baking powder
- ½ teaspoon vanilla extract

For the icing:

- 2 tablespoons protein powder
- 2 tablespoons almond milk
- 1 tablespoon melted coconut oil

Directions

1. Mix the protein powder, baking powder, almond meal and cinnamon. The smell of this last spice should bring a smile to everybody's faces.

2. Combine the other ingredients for the waffles and add them to the meal mixture.

3. Fire up the waffle iron. It is such an ancient and ubiquitous item that everyone is bound to have one hidden away somewhere.

4. When it is hot, pour the batter and cook until you get some golden waffles, just right for a nice, friendly conversation.

5. To prepare the frosting, mix the coconut oil with the protein powder and gradually add the milk.

6. Sprinkle some cinnamon over the waffles, and drizzle with the icing.

Eat immediately and don't leave even a single crumb on your plate.

These delicious waffles brought a smile to Missandei's face immediately. Grey Worm also tried to express his appreciation. He wasn't very convincing, but he promised to keep working on it.

BONE BROTH MISTAKES

Not all broths are made equal. Some folk have a special talent for creating these concoctions, while others produce mixtures that force us to smile through gritted teeth after tasting while we try to convince the cook that it doesn't completely suck. You know, like that smile Cersei gives Margaery every time they cross paths.

To ensure you stay on the queen's good side, be sure to avoid these 5 common mistakes. If you really want to hit the top of your game, take your learning further and keep refining your creations until you nail it.

There are plenty of great resources available, and there is nothing like a practiced eye and cultured tongue to guide you along.

1. Not Blanching

Always remember to blanch your bones before use. To do this, cover them with water and bring to the boil, cooking for approx. 18-20 minutes and then draining. Then they're ready for the next step, which is another common error.

Some folk even like to pre-soak the bones in vinegar and water before any heat is applied to draw out the goodness inside. You can add this step in first if you wish.

2. Not Roasting

Brown your bones at high heat in the oven so that they become caramelized (and super tasty) before you boil them. When boiling, some of this texture may come away, but try to capture it and use it for additional flavor.

You can do this by simply loosening the remainder with a wooden spatula or similar, and then placing it back into the broth.

3. Impatience

Big animals have big bones that require a lot of time to simmer. Don't cut it short, or you'll be missing out on all the flavors and goodness. Stick to the allotted time.

Smaller animals naturally take a shorter amount of time, but you should still allow it to pass before being tempted to haul your saucepan off the stove.

4. The Great Wait

As someone who has had to wait for a new series of Game of Thrones to be aired, you are clearly vastly experienced in exercising patience and therefore unlikely to make the previous mistake. But don't go too far the other way, either, as you could go past the point of peak goodness. The outer limits are generally between 36-48 hours depending on the cooking temperature. To be sure, just follow the recipe.

5. Cooling Off

Don't leave your broth to cool on the windowsill like mamma's homemade pie. Not only do you risk a cartoon cat coming along and stealing it, but you're also allowing bacteria to form. Instead, pop in a tray of ice cubes and transfer your creation to a wide, shallow container where it will cool quicker. Don't stick it straight in the fridge or freezer, as this again invites bacteria as well as heating everything else up inside!

"A WOMAN NEEDS COOKBOOKS LIKE A SWORD NEEDS A WHETSTONE."

MEASUREMENT CONVERSIONS

In ancient times, man measured with his hands. Then came cups, and many folk were content to stop there. Across the narrow sea, however, people were at work at work with a witchcraft they called 'metric'. To keep the peace, you will find common conversions between the units in the following sections.

LIQUIDS, HERBS & SPICES

Customary Quantity	Metric equivalent
1 teaspoon	5 mL
1 tablespoon *or* 1/2 fluid ounce	15 mL
1 fluid ounce *or* 1/8 cup	30 mL
1/4 cup *or* 2 fluid ounces	60 mL
1/3 cup	80 mL
1/2 cup *or* 4 fluid ounces	120 mL
2/3 cup	160 mL
3/4 cup *or* 6 fluid ounces	180 mL
1 cup *or* 8 fluid ounces *or* half a pint	240 mL
1 1/2 cups *or* 12 fluid ounces	350 mL
2 cups *or* 1 pint *or* 16 fluid ounces	475 mL
3 cups *or* 1 1/2 pints	700 mL
4 cups *or* 2 pints *or* 1 quart	950 mL
4 quarts *or* 1 gallon	3.8 L
Where precision is not justified, it may be convenient to round these conversions off as follows:	
1 cup = 250 mL	
1 pint = 500 mL	
1 quart = 1 L	
1 gallon = 4 L	

COMMON NON-LIQUIDS BY WEIGHT

Ingredient	1 cup	3/4 cup	2/3 cup	1/2 cup	1/3 cup	1/4 cup	2 Tbsp
Flour, all purpose (wheat)	120 g	90 g	80 g	60 g	40 g	30 g	15 g
Flour, well sifted all purpose (wheat)	110 g	80 g	70 g	55 g	35 g	27 g	13 g
Sugar, granulated cane	200 g	150 g	130 g	100 g	65 g	50 g	25 g
Confectioner's sugar (cane)	100 g	75 g	70 g	50 g	35 g	25 g	13 g
Brown sugar, packed firmly (but not too firmly)	180 g	135 g	120 g	90 g	60 g	45 g	23 g
Corn meal	160 g	120 g	100 g	80 g	50 g	40 g	20 g
Corn starch	120 g	90 g	80 g	60 g	40 g	30 g	15 g
Rice, uncooked	190 g	140 g	125 g	95 g	65 g	48 g	24 g
Macaroni, uncooked	140 g	100 g	90 g	70 g	45 g	35 g	17 g
Couscous, uncooked	180 g	135 g	120 g	90 g	60 g	45 g	22 g
Oats, uncooked quick	90 g	65 g	60 g	45 g	30 g	22 g	11 g
Table salt	300 g	230 g	200 g	150 g	100 g	75 g	40 g
Butter	240 g	180 g	160 g	120 g	80 g	60 g	30 g
Vegetable shortening	190 g	140 g	125 g	95 g	65 g	48 g	24 g
Chopped fruits and vegetables	150 g	110 g	100 g	75 g	50 g	40 g	20 g
Nuts, chopped	150 g	110 g	100 g	75 g	50 g	40 g	20 g
Nuts, ground	120 g	90 g	80 g	60 g	40 g	30 g	15 g
Bread crumbs, fresh, loosely packed	60 g	45 g	40 g	30 g	20 g	15 g	8 g
Bread crumbs, dry	150 g	110 g	100 g	75 g	50 g	40 g	20 g
Parmesan cheese, grated	90 g	65 g	60 g	45 g	30 g	22 g	11 g

WEIGHT CONVERSIONS

Customary Qty	Metric
1 ounce	28 g
4 ounces *or* 1/4 pound	113 g
1/3 pound	150 g
8 ounces *or* 1/2 pound	230 g
2/3 pound	300 g
12 ounces *or* 3/4 pound	340 g
1 pound *or* 16 ounces	450 g
2 pounds	900 g

"IF YOU THINK THIS HAS A HAPPY ENDING, YOU'RE CORRECT."

GET YOUR BONUS

Free Cookbooks

I'm always cooking, and love sharing my favorite recipes with friends and family. Occasionally I will even give entire cookbooks away for free to help spread the word and try out new ideas.

If you'd like to join my inner circle and receive free cookbooks just click the link below and I'll add you to my super secret list. Whenever I have a freebie available, you'll be the first to know!

Visit **http://geni.us/cookbookaddicts** to join the club now!

LIKE THIS BOOK?

These handsome scamps love their food just as much as I do! And they love hearing your feedback, too. OK, maybe that's just me.

Nothing makes me happier than hearing about your favorite recipes. If you'd like to share yours, please visit your Amazon purchase history to leave a quick review. I read every single one, and you can even upload a picture of your creations if you're feeling like a super big show-off!

Oh, and don't forget to tell a friend!

a Review Now!

Tweet 2,231

f Share 2k

ABOUT THE AUTHOR

Harper McKinney is head chef at the McKinney family, a self-confessed cookbook addict and huge Game of Thrones fan!

She enjoys nothing more than rustling something special up in the kitchen and sharing it with friends, families and total strangers alike.

Whether it be replicating a classic or inventing something totally new, McKinney loves sharing the results so that others can try their hand too.

She doesn't believe in cookbooks packed with fancy pictures, choosing instead to enjoy the act of creating something that is entirely unique, and the wonderful process of trial and error that comes with it.

The best way to learn is with a practiced eye and a cultured tongue, and the only way to obtain those is to get in the kitchen and get cracking. So, what are you waiting for?

To discover more wonderful cookbooks, just search 'Harper McKinney' on Amazon.

Printed in Great
Britain
by Amazon